Michael J. A McCaffery

THE SIEGE of SPOLETO

A camp-tale of Arlington Heights

Michael J. A McCaffery

THE SIEGE of SPOLETO
A camp-tale of Arlington Heights

ISBN/EAN: 9783741165085

Manufactured in Europe, USA, Canada, Australia, Japa

Cover: Foto ©Andreas Hilbeck / pixelio.de

Manufactured and distributed by brebook publishing software (www.brebook.com)

Michael J. A McCaffery

THE SIEGE of SPOLETO

THE

SIEGE OF SPOLETO;

A CAMP-TALE OF ARLINGTON HEIGHTS,

By MICHAEL J. A. McCAFFERY, M.A.

NEW-YORK:
P. O'SHEA, 104 BLEECKER ST.

1864.

Entered according to Act of Congress, in the year 1864,

By P. O'SHEA,

In the Clerk's Office of the District Court of the United States for the Southern District of New York.

TO

THE REVEREND FATHERS OF THE SOCIETY OF JESUS

The Faculty and Professors
OF
ST. JOHN'S COLLEGE, FORDHAM, NEW-YORK;

and also,

To my Fellow Students of the same Institution, scattered now

in every quarter of the Globe:

The following Lines,--

Meditated during some of the happy hours

we have spent together,—

are

Respectfully and Affectionately

INSCRIBED.

ERRATA.

Page 46, line 12th, for *arms*, read *hearts*.
Page 49, line 1st, for *leagured*, read *leaguered*.
Page 53, read the number of the stanza, *XXXI*.
Page 75, line 2d, for *father's*, read *fathers'*.

ARLINGTON HEIGHTS.

GLORIOUSLY fell the last mellow beams of the summer sun; placidly swept on to the sea the noble river; softly blushed in the sunset radiance the bold outline of stream and shore; and proudly, proudly as if in conscious power, floated above the scene our country's starry banner.

It was a picture, bright indeed and beautiful, but solemn and saddening in the associations which it suggested.

The American Government,—one of the best the world had ever seen,—had been threatened with overthrow. The national flag had been insulted, the national capital menaced with destruction. A fever of excitement pervaded the entire community. Commerce and manufactures were for a time suspended. Men of every class and station buckled on the sword and hastened to the defence of their common country. The cities of the North re-echoed to the incessant roll of the war-drum and to the tramp of armed thousands. The departing regiments marched through the streets amid the waving of scarfs and flags and the enthusiastic plaudits of the multitude. But grief and woe were in the hearts of many. The peace and happiness and lives of domestic circles were imperilled; and bereaved mothers, wives and children wept in vain for the loved ones stricken in their prime.

This state of things originated from no sudden or transient cause. Wounded passions had long rankled in the breast of the nation. The unnecessary interference of rabid fanatics in one section of the Union—which, indeed, had often partaken of the character of aggression—was met, in the other section, with haughty and defiant pride: the affections of each side were estranged, or deemed to be estranged, from the other: and the time had now come when the semblance of friendship and of a common citizenship was to be thrown aside, and the North and South were to stand, for a time at least, in the attitude of implacable foes.

Resenting the acts of individuals, or parties, as the acts of government, the Southerners had erected the standard of revolt. Armed bands had paraded through southern cities, and had concentrated at various points, avowedly for the purpose of destroying forever the last vestige of federal power.

South Carolina—always a firebrand in the Union—had taken the initiatory step in the work of disorganization: and around the federal fort in the harbor of Charleston, centred her battalions of angry men bent on trampling to the dust the flag that waved above its ramparts—the last emblem of constitutional authority.

For the first time in our history, the stars and stripes were dishonored by our own citizens. Fort Sumpter fell. With quivering lip and flashing eye the story of the insult was read on every hearthstone throughout the land; and, instantly, thousands of gallant men sprang forward to avenge it. Among those who early offered their services to the country in her hour of need were the members of the Sixty-Ninth Regiment, of New-York. Scarcely had the echo of Sumpter's cannon died away upon the breeze, ere around the crest of the now world-renowned ARLINGTON HEIGHTS, sprang up, as if by magic, beneath the sturdy arms of our Irish citizen soldier, a line of entrenchments bristling with cannon and shining bayonets.

For "the boys," as the soldiers of the Sixty-Ninth were familiarly styled, the expedition had proved no mere holiday parade. Since leaving their homes, their portion had been unceasing and arduous toil. Roads were to be constructed; communications between distant points opened and secured; enemies met and punished; property guarded; picket duty performed; a fort erected: and all this with scanty rations, and with no shelter from the drenching rains. And when their labors were completed, they were to be marched to the battle-field, and there left, with others equally unfortunate, without direction and without guidance, to the instincts of their own unquestioned but unavailing gallantry. Those who, with changing cheek, have read of the desperate charge of the Sixty-Ninth, twice repeated, up to the muzzles of the hostile guns that belched forth storms of grapeshot, need not be told that they nobly fulfilled their duty. Bravery, however, is not generalship, and — the Union troops were defeated. But to our story.

It was an evening in the middle of July, 1861, a few days before the BULL RUN disaster. The toils, the ceaseless parades and marches of the day were over; and, tired and jaded, "the boys" had cast themselves on the grass, in various easy postures, to enjoy an evening smoke ere the tattoo sounded to repose: and, as the last beams of the sun streamed over their bronzed faces and frayed uniforms, they presented a picture on whose varying lights and shades the pencil of a TITIAN would have loved to linger.

Among them all prevailed the easy familiarity and the thoroughly good understanding of men who had shared each other's hardships and tested each other's friendship in the hour of need, and who knew that, in similar hours, that friendship might be well relied on. Among them, too, circled the song and story, the mingling flow of humor and of pathos, the bright-flashing of the Irish mother wit and a perpetual cross-fire of mirth-provoking drollery. There was manifested, withal, and more particularly among the younger men, an eagerness for the fray, a longing restlessness to plunge into the excitement of the field, which their seniors sometimes found necessary to temper with cooler counsels.

A noble elm crowned one of the grassy knolls of the heights, and beneath its spreading boughs was gathered, on the evening I refer to, a picturesque group of five persons. Beneath them, and almost at their feet, stretched the broad expanse of the Potomac, unruffled by a breeze; while, in the distance, were to be seen the domes and spires of the capital, shining like molten gold.

"Come, let us sit down here! There, PHIL, is my pouch of tobacco—genuine Killikinick—pass it around! Fill up your pipes, my gay blades, and blaze away. We sha'n't be able to smoke much longer in the old fort, for I hear that we're ordered to be ready for marching at a moment's notice."

The speaker was a tall, well-formed personage, in the full flush of mature and manly strength. The easy and graceful bearing, not less than the stalwart form, and the frank countenance over which played an expression that might be taken as the consciousness of power, proclaimed him every inch a soldier. The buoyancy of spirit and, the rollicking deviltry that characterize the County of ——, well, not to particularize,—the County in Ireland where blackthornes are not accustomed to grow for nothing,—found a fair representative in

Private GLEESON.* But he gave way to hilarity only in particularly happy moments : his usual mood was one of quiet modesty and reserve. The person addressed was a younger man, of some twenty-five summers, of slight but muscular frame, whose usually animated countenance was now sobered with a melancholy listlessness. But the expression instantly changed as he answered :

"And I am glad to hear it, GLEESON, for I am tired of this hang-dog life we're leading — cooped up here like so many old hens. I do wish we were once sweeping over the battle-plain, the trumpets sounding to the charge."

---

* The thronging multitudes who have looked on the striking proportions of the gentlemen referred to, (and we hope to be excused for taking liberties with his name), as the Sixty-Ninth Regiment marched down Broadway, on leaving home for the seat of war, would, if they thought of the probable consequences of a charge of a body of such men on the battlefield, have re-echoed the encomium "Magnificent Tipperary!" The other names and characters of our story are, of course, entirely fictitious.

"And indeed it might be—*only* once !" said GLEESON.

"Very good for PHIL. BURKE," rejoined another; continue your nightly reading of 'Charley O'Malley,' my boy, and you'll daily improve your dare-devil spirit,—not that it needs improving, as it is !" The words were echoed from a clump of long grass, where the burly constitution of Lieutenant WILLIAM GRATTAN lay stretched at full length, while his meerschaum (WILL was partial to meerschaums) and the good-natured countenance at the end of it were enveloped in prodigious clouds of smoke. BURKE'S face was suffused with a faint flush; but the speaker continued with caustic dryness, "How grand it would be to head that celebrated charge—"

"Why, you great fat fellow," retorted, at length the young man, "it is consoling to know that if *you* can't charge you have only to be placed in the hottest of the battle, and you would be sure to

stand and fight—from sheer inability to run away.
But you are *not* the cold-blood you pretend to be:
ice girds the volcano: and it wants only the tap
of the war-drum to prove you, too, a heart of
flame."

"Poetic, too, eh? Well, well—poor fellow, from
my heart I pity you ;—overcome, quite, by moon-
light and 'Charley O'Malley' ?"

A half-joking, half-indignant rejoinder sprang to
the lips of BURKE; but just then chimed in Corporal
TONE. The Corporal was a dapper little gentleman,
in an excruciatingly tight jacket. He was afflicted
with one or two little eccentricities. He could
never keep a secret: and every fact, or incident,
or harmless piece of news he happened to hear,
he evinced a decided propensity to transmit to
his neighbor with extemporized circumstances of
the most aggravated character. In short, to use

a very vulgar but very expressive word, the Corporal was a "blower."

"Here, boys," he said, sinking his voice to an ominous whisper; "this is between ourselves, though,—so don't let it go further,—we are going to march to-morrow. The rebels have advanced four hundred thousand strong! All the pickets are driven in! The enemy are sweeping everything before them with fire and sword! The President is in dismay! Consternation reigns in the Cabinet —and we are going to hold the enemy in check till reinforce———"

"T–h–e d–e–u–c–e!" ejaculated Bob Sheridan, with well-affected horror, and Bob grinned "a ghastly, horrid smile," that would have made one's heart melt. "Sweeping all before them with fire and sword! And the Sixty-Ninth to be thrown as a sop into the all-devouring maw of the enemy! Signal honor—great day for the Irish!"

"Aye, Bob, it *is* a great day for the Irish," answered Phil. Burke, seriously, though he laughed at Bob's antic. "A great day, truly, when the Sixty-Ninth, and other regiments of foreign-born citizens, are the hope of the country. There will be less of the anti-foreign spirit rampant in America; for the 'foreign element,' as it is called, has evinced a hearty willingness to defend the Constitution and the Union. And if there be a chord of gratitude in the great American heart, the alacrity with which the 'Exiles of Erin,' among others, leaped forth to preserve the country of Washington, will not be soon or easily forgotten. I hope, however, we shall have an occasion to show more than *mere willingness.*"

"Right, Phil, right," returned Bob; "but," and another grin lightened across his features from ear to ear, " I wonder if the Corporal here won't prove his title to his country's gratitude in a signal manner."

"He will, I dare be sworn—when he goes home!" echoed Lieutenant GRATTAN—and the smoke-wreathes twined vigorously from the tall grass up through the leafy branches overhead: but, through the smoke, down near the turf, a pair of great large eyes twinkled mischievously.

"But, GLEESON," said PHIL, "what about your long-promised STORY OF SPOLETO? We couldn't have a better time and place for it than the present. We have an hour to while away yet, so begin."

"I never tell *stories*," said GLEESON, quietly.

"Why," said the Lieutenant, "I would prefer to hear the Corporal tell it: GLEESON, you know, need but give him the *chief points!*"

The urgent and friendly solicitations of all finally prevailed over GLEESON's unwillingness.

"It is a subject," he said, "in which we are all peculiarly interested. The same idea,—the inviolability of legitimate government,—that we are striving to uphold here, the Irish fought for in Italy. If there be no stability of government,—if constitutions are toys, to be changed or abolished at every whim,—there is not, and there cannot be, any security for the governed.

"They said that GARIBALDI was coming over here to take command of a part of the Union forces' But the Italian Filibuster is more consistent. He could not very well fight in Italy for insurrection and rebellion, and in America for authority and conservatism.

"But I feel that I am unable to speak, as one ought to speak, of affairs in Italy. When I think of them, even now, my veins thrill with unwonted pulses: and the thoughts that come rushing on my mind beggar utterance. Ah, if I could only *express* what

I *feel!* But I rely on you to supply my defects. Where my words are cold make them of fire;— where they are dull make them to ring clear as a clarion battle-note;—and where I but sketch the outline, do you fill up the lights and shades."

THE SIEGE OF SPOLETO.

I.

Scarce piercing the blue mists of morn
the beaming sun came down
Upon the crumbling ramparts of Spoleto's
leaguered town;
From tower and swelling dome, from the
old Cathedral spire
From scarfs, and flags, and bristling arms,
glanced back the golden fire.
One standard flaunts it proudly above the
stirring scene;
And Erin's shamrocks glisten o'er its field
of glorious green:
And gallant hearts beneath it thrill with
wildest joy to-day,
And smiling lips breathe words of deep
impatience for the fray.

II.

They come as to a festival; they gather side by side,
The reaper from his golden grain, the bridegroom from his bride;
The stripling, and the veteran with wealth of snowy locks,
The artist from his easel, and the student from his books.
And what has lured them hither from their distant ocean isle?
And why wears every blooming cheek so proud, so bright a smile?
Can they thus rush to battle, nor grieve that they may die?
Can they face the king of terrors, and smile,—and he so nigh?

III.

'Twas no dream of martial glory,—though
    that perhaps were dear;
'Twas not to live in story, through many
    a coming year;
'Twas no ambitious wish for power, no
    tempting of red gold,
No wiles of syren pleasure that their
    bosoms brave controlled.
No!—nobler thoughts than wealth, or
    fame, or power, or pleasure's charm,
Inspire each lofty hero-heart and nerve
    each warrior-arm;
'Twas the spirit that of old had led the
    lances of the West
To redeem from sacrilegious hands the
    land a Saviour blest

IV.

Had ye seen them on that morn, as they
    knelt around the shrine,[1]
Ere yet the first faint beams of dawn
    stole o'er the Appenine,
When with censers high up-swinging and
    with tapers gleaming bright,
And with solemn anthems ringing, went
    on the holy rite,—
Had ye marked how reverently they bent
    to receive the sacred food,
Joy brightening o'er each feature, as they
    there communed with God,—
Ye had said that there was worship, such
    as only hearts can give
That for a noble purpose struggle, for a
    noble purpose live.

V.

And when the sacred rites were o'er, and
the choristers were gone,
And the tapers on the altar were extin-
guished one by one,—
When the bugle, winding loud and shrill,
called each one to his post,—
And dark as lowering thunder-clouds,
stormed on the leaguering host,
Oh! had ye seen them then, as rushed the
foeman in his pride,
How, like ocean rocks, they towered and
rolled back the battle's tide,
Ye had said that there was valor, such
as only heroes feel,
When in a high and holy cause they grasp
the avenging steel.

VI.

They tell us that the golden age of chivalry is o'er,
That lives in no brave bosom now the lofty soul of yore,
When, rallying round the Cross, to arms all banded Europe sprang,
And Juda's plains with feats of might and knightly prowess rang.
They tell us that the glories of those days have passed away;
And hearts that would have throbbed for fame now sleep with kindred clay;
That no gallant deeds of arms are done to make the bosom thrill,—
And but the Past's bright memories around us linger still.

VII.

But the glories of the Age of Faith, whatever bigots say,
Its valor, constancy and worth, have not all passed away:
Still lives the same high spirit as in the olden time,
When loyalty was virtue, and when cowardice was crime.
Still are deeds of valor done, not unworthy other days;
Still proud trophies nobly won, to claim undying praise;
Still are blent in hero-breasts, the patriot fire of Brian,[2]
The piety of Godfrey, and the might of Cœur-de-Lion.

VIII.

For still there lives a lofty, active, soul-inspiring power,
That calls forth all of great and good, as Spring calls forth the flower;
That raises man above distress, and fear, and woe, and death,
The noblest gift of heaven to earth,—our ever-glorious faith!
And that faith had ne'er burned brighter than in the breasts of those,
Who gather on Italian plains to combat 'gainst its foes:
And that faith has made bold heroes of the veteran and the youth,—
Of the simple hearts of Erin, the stern champions of truth.

IX.

They had heard afar in Erin, how base
    minions sought to rend,
In anger from the placid brow of their
    father, priest and friend,
The triple crown, which ages in its lustre
    had bequeathed,
And a line of saints and sages with glory's
    halo wreathed.
They had seen an old man on his throne
    confront the robber hordes,
And meet, with tranquil smiles alone, the
    threats of guilt-stained swords;
They had seen how nations round him had
    betrayed, deserted, sold,—
And alas, they knew, perchance too well,
    the power of England's gold.

X.

But enough that they are Irish, to do
    battle for the faith,
Nor reck, as its defenders, aught of
    danger, aught of death!
In generous rivalry they come and snatch
    the indignant sword,
To avenge the outraged Vicar of the God
    their sires adored.
They stand forth there for Pius, a bulwark
    firm arrayed,
With hearts exultant leaping to think
    that they can aid;
And ere *his* heart were wrung by aught
    that slight or scorn implied,
Their gallant breasts had joyed to drain
    their life-blood's warmest tide.

XI.

"Say that our only hopes are on the
    prompt relief he sends;
And hasten to our side the fearless bay-
    onets of our friends:
Till your return, at every cost, we keep
    the foe at bay;
If not,—then we are proud to die:—
    enough! God speed! away!"
The youth looks up with mantling cheek
    and learns his mission high;
Thanks for his chief's confiding trust, his
    grateful smiles imply;
His crest upflings as he lightly springs to
    the back of his milk-white steed,
And clattering echoes wake again his
    courser's tramp of speed.[a]

XII.

Brave defenders of the Pope, now look
    your last upon God's sun,—
For its rays shall gild your ashes, ere this
    summer day be done!
Your foes press round on every side, like
    blood-hounds on the trail,
As countless as the rustling leaves when
    autumn strews the gale.
They ask and *give* no quarter—they wield
    no sparing brand,—
And will exercise scant mercy towards
    your hardy little band :—
Mercy! Call for mercy on the tigress in
    her rage,—
Not on those who glut their vengeance
    on defenceless sex and age!

XIII.

For look! where, mustering o'er the plain,
    their splendid thousands come,
With tramp of steeds, and clash of arms
    and spirit-stirring drum.
Their rushing squadrons shake the ground
    as they wheel, deploy and form,
And deep their trundling cannon sound,
    like mutterings of the storm.
Far o'er the field, from right to left, their
    bristling lines extend,
And with the leafy forest in the hazy
    distance blend:
And now,—broods o'er their marshalled
    ranks a stillness deep and dead,
As that, which ere the tempest burst, inspires prophetic dread.

XIV.

How beautiful! In splendor sweeping
along the bright array,
From point to point of bayonets leaping,
the glittering sunbeams play,
Her smiling beauties o'er the field fair
Nature wide unveils:
The grassy plains and clustered groves
and vine-embowered dales,
The trees that make soft music to the
rippling of the rill,
The sloping lawn far-spreading and the
distant vine-clad hill,
In the glory of the vintage, shining purple from afar,
All,—lend enchantment to the cold stern
pageantry of war.

XV.

One horseman rides from out their midst
    and spurs across the field,
The bearer of a flag of truce and sum-
    mons stern to yield;
And brief his words, as drawing rein
    before the little band,
His gaze as if to note each thought, their
    features sharply scanned:
"Now yield ye prisoners of war, to our
    all-conquering host;—
For the genius of our country, rising
    proudly from the dust,
Comes forth in native majesty, from bon-
    dage, woes and tears,
To avenge on tyrant priest-craft the in-
    dignities of years!"

XVI.

Then forth stood brave O'Reilly, for his soul could scantly brook
The envoy's deep insulting words, his pride of tone and look;
"Ye prate of wrongs" he said, "and woes that crush Italia down:
Who wastes the field? or sacks the cot? or desolates the town?
Who tracks the land with battle's fires, and havoc's dreadful signs—
Dishonored daughters, slaughtered sires, and desecrated shrines?
Not priest-craft!—but the sons Italia nurtured at her breast,
That, viper-like, have turned and stung the hand that once caressed."

XVII.

"Of the genius of your country, ye speak
   in lofty phrase,—
Of her blighted hopes and fortunes, of
   her fame in ancient days:—
And who have crowned your clime with
   fame, in every passing age,
And emblazoned with their glorious names
   her story's brightest page?
Not ye,—who tear the *priest* and *monk*
   from out their cloistral homes,[4]
Destroy their gems of pictured art, and
   burn their cherished tomes,—
Who have hushed their voice of learning
   in their far-famed classic halls,
And left mementos of your hate in black-
   ened smouldering walls."

XVIII.

"But truce to strife of idle words! time
    presses to be brief:—
Ride back then with our thanks, sir, for
    this warning of your chief:
We trust our swords ere night shall prove
    his courtesies were showered
Upon no base dishonored slave, no craven-
    hearted coward.
Go back, and tell your comrades to pause
    ere yet too late,
Nor with crime-laden souls to tempt a
    soldier's sudden fate:
For some, who would their traitor hands
    in sovereign's blood imbrue,
A soldier's death shall this day cheat
    the gallows of its due."

XIX.

The courier sneering listened, but answer
    deigned he none ;
Then haughtily turned bridle-rein and like
    a thought was gone.
The young chief, pondering, paused the
    while as shoutings rent the air,
That told how true he spoke the will of
    the brave souls gathered there.
The warm blood in its eloquent play surged
    o'er his manly cheek,
While at his heart stirred mighty thoughts
    no lip might fitly speak ;
A loftier mien his features wore than
    graces courts or thrones,
As once again his voice rang out its stir-
    ring trumpet tones :

XX.

"Sons of Patrick! Sons of Erin! oh, what
    memories of the past
To-day, in light around me here, their
    golden glories cast:
They paint the patriot's daring deeds and
    scenes of fame unfold,
Where deep our fathers' falchions struck
    for faith in days of old.
Like winds that wake the slumbering harp,
    they thrill my eager soul,
And every chord that vibrates there obeys
    their wild control;
They breathe the strain that high resolve
    and constancy inspires,
And tune each wayward impulse to the
    triumphs of our sires."

XXI.

"Shall we make our guiding battle-star,
nor follow where it beam—
Like gage of knightly honor, shall we
pledge and not redeem—
These memories of our gallant sires who
loved their ancient faith,
And proved that love, through years of
wrong, in danger and in death?
Their spirits are around us in the mingling
flame and smoke,—
Shall they not know their children by the
lightning of their stroke?
What though the foeman wields a score,
where our blades count but one?[5]
Be nerved, our hearts! Strike deep, our
swords! Their guilty course is run."

XXII.

"The stranger lords it proudly in our
    ancient castle halls,
The harp that once breathed triumph-
    strains 'hangs mute on Tara's walls,'
The banner that once proudly shone in
    CLONTARF'S sun of fame,—
Whose every flash was conquest,— is a
    thing of scorn and shame:
And captive Erin can but waft loved bles-
    sings o'er the wave,
For them to whom her tyrant would deny
    a peaceful grave:
E'en *mind* is exiled from the land where
    Genius set her throne:
King, country, flag, home, wealth, name,
    fame,—all, save our faith is gone."

XXIII.

"But that,—unlike the glories of the
  massive sculptured pile
That lends a ruined grandeur to each
  hill-top of our isle,—
Yet stands! a nobler monument than
  abbey-dome or tower,—
One the spoiler cannot desecrate, nor
  brunt of time o'erpower.
'Tis now our only heritage,—our pride,—
  our flower,—our gem,—
The one lone jewel that remains of Erin's
  diadem;
Shall it have blazed so bright, so long,
  upon her peerless brow,
And we do aught to dim its sheen or mar
  its beauty now?

XIV.

"Hope beams brightly on your faces,
    proudly swell your hearts to-day,
And wild with joy along each vein the life-
    blood currents play;
Our proudest hour has come; it makes
    the privilege our own,
Of guarding from the Oppressor's tread
    the steps of Pius' throne:
And if we are to fall to-day,—for num-
    bers may prevail,
And, worn with toil, strong arms may flag,
    and gallant arms may fail,—
Bequeathing to our country's care our
    memory and our names,—
Let e'en our death assert the rights eter-
    nal justice claims."

XXV.

A hundred hostile cannon boomed the
onset far and wide;
A proud defiance ringing back three hundred cheers replied;
The foemen trained their heavy guns upon
the old low walls,
And from afar, like pattering hail, rained
fast their storm of balls.
The bombshell, like a thing of doom, a
moment hung in air,
Then down upon its track of fate careered
with meteor glare;
And where,—the thunderbolt of war,—
it blighting, withering, sped,
There fire and death and ruin reigned,
and life and beauty fled.

XXVI.

Around the walls the leagured guns in
    irksome silence lay,[6]
Their range too short to answer back the
    foeman's iron play.
The Irish on the rampart can but pace
    their ball-swept round,
While at their feet the battle-sleet tears,
    up the mouldy ground.
And as red Slaughter walks their midst,
    and ruins yawn to seize,
They fret and chafe, like mettled steeds
    that snuff the battle breeze:
Nor reck they of the bolts of death as
    fast and far they fly,
For death can bring no terror to those
    prepared to die.

XXVII.

The batteries of the foe are wrapped as
    in a smoky shroud;
Their sheeted fires leap out at times, like
    lightning from a cloud;
The vollied thunder peal on peal the hills
    like playthings shake,
And in a hundred caverned cells the
    mountain echoes wake:
And ringing, shattering, crashing loud, the
    chain-shot sweeps the town,
And tower and parapet are rent, and
    massive walls go down:
The bursting shells would make the town
    its champions' funeral pyre,
While o'er a hundred mansions waves the
    blood-red flag of fire.

XXVIII.

For hours the crumbling ramparts fell
    beneath the angry balls,
For hours the circling band of fire swept
    closer to the walls;
And now the rolling drum tells where the
    gathering foemen form,
And onward press, in columned mass, the
    guarded breach to storm.
It is the post of danger—and brave Ire-
    land's sons are there,—
And mow down marshalled ranks beneath
    their rifles' sheeted glare:
But though they bear the battle's brunt
    unmoved as storm-swept rock,
Nor arm nor breast might long withstand
    the foe's resistless shock,

XXIX.

Shall structured bankment hope to stem
    the rushing torrent's flow?
Shall e'en the forest king not bend when
    raging tempests blow?
The little band, 'mid numbers lost—what
    though their arms they plied?—
Dashed back like veriest playthings in
    that whelming human tide—
Borne hither—thither—bent and swayed
    amid the frenzied throng,—
With rifle-shot and bayonet-thrust the
    hopeless fight prolong;
Though spent with toil, begrimed with dust
    and sweltering noontide heat,—
Fast fall their foes to rise no more along
    their slow retreat.

XXX.

There stood two brothers⁷ in the breach,
    where low the shattered wall,
A shapeless, yawning, ruined mass, had
    crumbled in its fall:
The bearded lip and swarthy cheek, firm
    eye and toil-knit form,
Told one,—who o'er life's troubled sea
    had battled many a storm:
The other,—a bright blue-eyed boy; less
    fit to haunt the camp,
Than high to swell a mother's joy, or trim
    the student's lamp:
A native manliness and grace sat on his
    lofty brow,
And tempered o'er the youthful face that
    played in smiles below.

X I.

A common impulse fired their breasts and
  lured them to the field,
To urge the fight for truth and right, and
  age from insult shield:
Bright beaming in the ranked array their
  plumes united shone,
And where their brother swords fell fast,
  their strokes flashed out as one:
And where, with flowing flaxen locks, that
  well craved gentle ruth,
In all the wanton hardihood of bold impetuous youth,
The fearless stripling wayward led,—there
  struggled at his side,
A brother's arm to share the stroke or
  fate that might betide.

XXXII.

When fiercest raged the conflict, and gathered maddened men
In angry vortex of the strife, high flashed their sabres then;
And winged with bright-plumed victory, and stained with dripping red
Built high around their gory steps a breastwork of the dead.
But as they wage the unequal fight, the stripling hero reels—
And faint and dizzy,—sick at heart,—a palor o'er him steals;—
A vengeful wound upon his breast, whence coursed a crimson flood,
Told where the ringing rifle-ball drank deep his heart's best blood.

XXXIII.

He sinks to earth and o'er his brow the
　　death-dews gather cold,—
But e'en in death his hand retains its
　　faithful sabre's hold:
His swimming eye no longer marked who
　　eased his drooping head,
But hand seeks hand in brother clasp and
　　loving words are said:
The memory of the dying boy sweeps
　　back to other hours;—
His spirit treads again the paths of child-
　　hood's sunny bowers;
Again to earn a mother's praise he tasks
　　each childish wile,
And o'er his face in beauty beams a calm
　　sweet wondrous smile.

XXXIV.

"Poor mother—tell her. Frank,—her boy
   no recreant coward died—
She cannot grieve—in such a cause—"
   and then a gushing tide
Chokes all his accents struggling warm
   through death's last parting chill;
"God—brother!—" bubbles o'er his lips,
   —one pang—and all is still.
Gone—while the thundering cannon peal
   his mournful requiem dirge;
Gone—while the valiant sink, like wrecks,
   in the battle's rolling surge;
Gone—with his bright young spirit robed
   in innocence and love,
To choir with kindred angels in the victor
   bands above.

XXXV.

The strong man bowed him o'er the boy,
of care unconscious now,
Swept back the soft bright sunny curls
that clustered round his brow,
Gently composed the rigid limbs, the little
hands caressed,
And on his marble lips a long last parting
tribute pressed.
No moisture dims his frenzied eye—too
deep his grief for tears—
But o'er him in that moment surged the
bitterness of years;
No trace his iron mien betrays of the
fires that heart-deep glow,
Save the wrung brow darkening sternly
in wild agony of woe.

XXXVI.

Who guards unwearied vigil, lest intruding
    hostile tread
Profane the grassy couch where sleeps the
    lowly-lying dead?
And through the long hours of the fight,
    whose rifle, ringing wide,
Told, as the unerring bullet sped,—not
    unavenged he died?
And when with anger stung, he leaped
    where clashing ranks entwined,
Whose arm tore on like heaven's bolt,—
    and ruin stalked behind?—
Ye might know him by his brother's plume,
    as through the ranks he strode,—
By his sword that slaked its vengeance in
    atoning streams of blood.

XXXVII.

Loud echoing through the narrow streets
    discordant clamors ring,
And fiercely on opposing swords opposing
    warriors spring :
The gale now swears "a death to priests"
    as loud the Italians cry;
"Our God and Pope!" now Ireland's stern
    deep slogan tones reply,
Dim rolling clouds of smoke now veil, and
    shifting, now reveal
The jarring shock, the shattering arms,
    and cold bright flash of steel ;
While good swords, shivering to the grasp,
    the mingled uproar drown
As foemen grappling, part no more, till
    one or both go down.

XXXVIII.

In vain the myriad foemen rush, like
    wolves upon the prey;
In vain their rifles' ready ring, and sabres'
    vengeful sway:
Their columns leap like torrents down,—
    again,—again,—again!—
Like foam dashed back, they fall before
    that handful of brave men.
The anguished cry, the dying moan on
    every side resound,
And crimson dead with hand still clenched
    bestrew the cumbered ground:
While victory to the Irish, to their foes
    defeat, presage,
The cheery shout of triumph and the
    shriek of baffled rage,

XXXIX.

O'Reilly bears him bravely amid the deepening fight,
And where the war-clouds darkest lower, his sword makes stormy light.
His snowy plume floats gaily, as he rushes to the fray,
Like vulture, hovering, ere it stoop adown upon the prey.
O God!—how terrible the might that mails the warrior's arm,
When, fighting in a sacred cause, high hopes his bosom warm!
Like eagle sporting 'mid the storms and lightnings of the skies,
He glories in the peril and the shafts of death defies.

XL.

Now kindling high with triumph, now bright with anger's blaze,
His wary eye oft keenly threads the battle's changing maze;
Detects the foe's concealed intent, ere yet 'tis ripely planned,
And flashes forth the signal-glance that tells—*where*—*how*—withstand!
Quick at his lead, his troops combined confront the baffled foe,
Now here, now there, with crushing force anticipate the blow;
Now sternly charge where headlong pours the foeman's threatening might,
And turn his fancied triumph to defeat and dastard flight.

XLI.

High in the beamy noontide rays a thousand sabres flash;
Like meteors through the echoing streets a thousand coursers dash:
Bright plumes and manes are blending, as each horseman bends him low,
With form all crouched, and nerve all strung, to leap upon the foe.
Down, down, with hoof of lightning and with thunder-ringing tramp,
Stretch the bounding steeds, besprent with foam;—the bit they madly champ;
Down, down, speed the headlong troopers;
—the bugle fires them on,—
But little reck they whither, so the strife and spoil be won:

XLII.

Down on the living rampart, like a brattling thunder peal,
Where the Irish tower athwart their path, a wall of bristling steel:—
Oh God!—how many a deep-gashed steed has reeled to the clanging pave,
Or rider swept to his final charge, swung his last battle-glaive!
Ha! will ye hound the hunted stag, till he turn and stand at bay?
Back,—ere he rend your toils like webs, your mirth dash with dismay!
They falter! they reel!—one vollied peal and away like mist they melt;
"Now!—Charge!"—the shout like thunder out, burst from the maddened Celt.

XLIII.

So ever stand the champion band that
dare defend the right!
So tower truth's bulwark phalanx mid the
terrors of the fight!
So, blenching from the battle-shock recoil
the banded foe,
And break, as breaks upon the rock, the
ocean's billowy flow!
Unsheathed for truth and justice, reek,
reek, falchions, to the hilt!
Nor list the voice of mercy now, for mercy
now were guilt!
And what though carnage riot o'er a
field where none survives?
Worse one truth lost forever than a hundred thousand lives.[9]

XLIV.

Red was the drip of levelled steel, as black
    with dust and gore,
'Mid plunging steeds, o'er trampled men
    the charging Irish tore:
On, on they crash, mid falling wrecks, and
    the battle's sulphurous breath,
Nor mark they now the writhing pang
    and the white eyes' glare of death.
There is fever in each vein, there is frenzy
    in each heart,
And memories o'er each throbbing brain,
    like angry spectres, start,
And sternly ask to be avenged; Revenge,
    how grimly sweet!
And Erin's sons that day in blood retrieve
    each past defeat.

XLV.

The stifled moan, the gurgling groan, the sob, the suppliant cry,
The pallid cheek, the nerveless arm, the throe of agony;
The gasping courser lying o'er his rider stiff and cold;
The mangled dead and dying in crimson masses rolied;
Limbs shattered, corslets rent, guns, swords, on every side bestrewed,
And tattered pennons dabbling in pools of clotted blood;
All, all,—grim War, abashed to look where fell his last dread stroke,
In pity shrouds the horrid scene in winding-sheet of smoke.

XLVI.

Yet, Erin, though thy bayonets gleam in
    triumph o'er the dead,
Thy labored step and ebbing strength
    declare thou too hast bled;
But not yet droop thy toil-spent arm, nor
    faint thy gallant heart,—
For where one foe went redly down a
    thousand freshly start!
Around thee deepening war-clouds lower,
    —dark, darker still, their gloom,
Their lightnings glare to rend thy breast,
    their thunders speak thy doom;
Back!—till the castle round thee its shel-
    tering rampart spread,—
Back!—ere the mustering eagles stoop to
    banquet on thy dead!

XLVII.

Oh for a thousand arms like theirs, where
 the lark-loved daisies blow,
In that sad hour to launch their might
 upon the whelming foe!
Not then from wearied Valor's brow had
 Number snatched the wreath:
Not then had Erin's conquered sword in
 sorrow sought its sheath.
Aye, were but a thousand banded there,
 how had they leaped to shield
The dauntless band that well could die,
 but knew not how to yield!
Aye, had they marked that firm retreat,
 that tearful keen despair,
How had they proud redeemed it into
 glorious triumph there!

XLVIII.

Now proudly dealing stroke for stroke, and answering fire for fire,
In turn, before their rallying foes, the Irish slow retire;
Closer their thinned ranks binding, they wrest a backward way,
And, still retreating, sternly keep their countless foes at bay.
As rage the mountain billows round the bark they would submerge,
As, plunging bravely on, that bark o'ertops the billowy surge,—
So, round the weary hero-band, up-springing legions swell,
So, flinging back the foe, they gain the sheltering citadel.

XLIX.

Respite again—brief, but enough to wring
    the mutual hand,
Enough to speak the parting word, to
    whet the deadliest brand!
For, as the clashing gate swept to, and the
    green flag climbed on high,
They knew that they had taken then a
    last stand there—to die!
The dear green flag,—a thing of pride—
    they watched it graceful rise,
And as it flung a beautiful defiance from
    the skies,
The pent-up passion of their breasts, a
    cheer, a ringing cheer
Proclaimed that when it fell 'twould twine
    its last defender's bier.

E.

Again rides forth a flag of truce, stern
 triumph on his brow;
O'Reilly's answering features wore no
 haughtier smile than now:
"Indignant, back we proudly fling, demand,
 threat, insult,—all;—
While sword can smite or arm can swing,
 our Pope ye shall not thrall;
With freedom's watchword on your lips,
 ye draw the rebel glaive
Against the Church that ransomed home
 the captive and the slave.[9]
But written in high heaven our oath, to
 fall if not defend her:—
In such a cause an Irishman can die, but
 not surrender!"[10]

LI.

Then poured the red artillery forth the
    death-winged battle-sleet,—
Then spread the smoke above the dead,
    their only winding sheet,—
Then ceaseless rushed the cannon balls,
    sped by relentless hate,
Where centred all the hostile guns—the
    iron castle gate.
It trembles like a frighted thing,—it rocks
    and sways amain,—
It yields! it yields!—one long last writhe,
    one struggle, one mighty strain,
And tottering, toppling, crashing down,—
    a massive ruin all,—
Sink smoking to the quaking earth, gate,
    parapet, and wall.

LII.

Like shaft from string, like stone from
    sling, the columned foe is sped,[11]
Flung sternly back, and bayonet-riven,
    their corslets stream with red;
Two cannon mounted in the breach, by
    lusty sinews plied,
Oft plough a dead-strewn passage through
    the ever-rushing tide.
Again, like spectres through the smoke,
    across the bridge they spring,
And bayonets reek, and the falling shriek,
    and the deadly cannon ring;
And then, but not till then, the breach,
    the well-fought breach is won,
When falls the last brave cannonier athwart
    his empty gun.

LIII.

Won? No! a remnant yet remains to die
    for their father's faith;—
And as they close with their victor foes
    in the last stern clasp of death,
Like fire glares out each wrath-lit eye,
    and each arm is braced like steel,
And sweat-drops stream from the bursting
    brow, in the strife as they writhe and reel.
Vain, vain the sheen of hostile sword, and
    glittering breast-plate's charm,
When vengeance wakes the soul that sleeps
    in the hero's death-girt arm!
Hurled from the rampart fall the foe,—
    like leaves from wintry bough:—
The stream that coursed the castle-foss—
    what chokes its current now?

LIV.

Hushed are the thunders of the fight, the
    din and clangor cease—
And War, disarmed, abates his front before
    the smile of Peace!
For lo! his milk-white charger, and his
    helmet's flowing plume—
Know ye not yet that grateful smile and
    that cheek of youthful bloom?
'Tis he who spurred that morn for aid, his
    comrade's only hope,—
Returning now in loftier guise—the herald
    of the Pope;
And foes—they know he ends a strife for
    them perchance too keen!
And friends—his soldier's courtesy return
    with kindly mien.

LV.

As slow he climbs the dead-strewn slope
and gains the ruined gate,
His tidings high with anxious hearts the
Irish calm await;
From every lip the queried tones "And
come our comrades?" flow;
But trembling hope is crushed again,—the
envoy answers "No!

Fast sped my steed 'neath whip and spur—
at noon I reached the Pope,
And craved five—three—one—thousand
men, that we might fairly cope—"
"And would your band so dare withstand
the far-outnumbering foe?"
"Aye, till they drain from every vein its
life-blood's ruddiest flow."

LVI.

"Oh then, my chief, had you but seen
how sad the Pontiff wept,
While o'er his face a soul-lit smile of pleased
emotion swept,—
And heard his words, so kind, so warm,
so full of noble pride,
You had not changed that tribute rare for
aught on earth beside.
'Speed back—no aid is mine to send,—
back! end the hopeless fight,—
The remnant save from an early grave, ere
the foeman's sword shall smite;
Thanks, thanks,—but poor and cold the
word,—to the still surviving band,—
But bid them yield the well-fought field,
and say *I* ask!—command!'"

LVII.

More keen those words than hostile swords!
—To yield, but not to die,
To live to see the old flag swept in conquest from the sky,
To tame the bounding Celtic blood, the triumph to forego,
To feel the exultant rapture of a proud malignant foe;—
This wrung their souls with torture! but the mandate was obeyed,—
In tears—by men who had withstood the death-charge undismayed
Sad, silent, slow, disarmed they go, while round them foemen throng,
To view the band,—of captives now,—who braved their power so long.

LVIII.

Captives—but not for long in chains or
    dungeon-cell to pine ;
He breaks their bonds, to guard whose
    throne their lives they would resign ;
Exchanged—but sworn to fight no more,
    —they trim the homeward sail,
That o'er the lightly-bounding wave bends
    to the favoring gale.
Home to the father's hearthstone,—to the
    mother, daughter, bride!
Home to the friends of those who fell,
    and tell them how they died!
Home to a nation's blessing, in a chorus-
    peal that starts,
And the "hundred thousand welcomes"
    from a hundred thousand hearts.

LIX.

And in revolving years, that steal the
arm's once sinewy power,
When round the earth the household
meet as evening shadows lower,
When voices, tuned to melody, ring out
the music-chime,
And legend-lore lends pinions to the too-
fast flight of time,
Then as the children climb the knee, and
lisp Spoleto's name,
Then, let their hearts go thrilling to the
story of your fame ;—
Then sow the seeds that sleep perchance,
but soon or late shall bear,
Bright hero-laurels, fadeless as the glory-
wreathes ye wear.

LX.

Though now loved Erin droops and pines
  while tyrant chains oppress,—
Though captive bows her tameless soul to
  sorrow and distress,—
Though oft in plaintive prayer she grieves,
  as tears of anguish flow,—
In prayer counts o'er to God alone the
  decades of her woe ;—
Not long, until her dark, dark night,—its
  tears,—its woes have passed ;
Not long, till strikes the glorious hour
  when dawn breaks forth at last ;
Not long, till through the darkness beams
  the herald-star of day,
And deep, and deeper flushing, bursts the
  morning's dazzling ray !

LXI.

O, morn of brightest rapture!—with its
 pictured glories teem
The wanderer's exile-wrested sigh and
 patriot-haunting dream;
And, longing each to catch its ray,—with
 blades upflung in air,—
In every clime along the earth, unnumbered
 falchions glare.
As throng the serried ocean waves, that,
 —far as eye can sweep,—
From every side to greet thy shore, in
 flashing splendor leap,
So, Erin, on that morning, from across
 the sounding sea,
Shall throng steel-crested legions of deliv-
 erers to thee.

LXII.

Then, then, at last, a long-furled flag, to
    freedom's breeze unrolled,
In graceful pride flings boldly free each
    brilliant emerald fold:
Then, then, a sweet sad harp unbinds each
    sorrow-muffled string,
And, thrilling deep, its wildest tones a
    triumph anthem ring:
Then, bright as youthful morning, crowned
    and sceptred as a queen,
Uprisen in new-born majesty, joy mantling
    o'er her mien,
Loved Erin comes, while prayers and hopes
    in myriad hearts have birth,
And proudly "takes her place among the
    nations of the earth."

The full moon was by this time high on her unclouded path: her rays shimmered tremulously down through the elm leaves, and shone in chequered spots on the dark sward and on the group that sat there, thoughtful, silent, stilling the quick-swelling pulses of their hearts, while cheeks kindled and eyes flashed in her soft light.

Had the speaker desired applause, that silence were applause enough: but it became oppressive to him at length, and turning to one of his comrades, he said:

"Come, WILL, let us have a song; 'turn about is fair play,' you know."

Without any affected unwillingness, the Lieutenant complied. With the tumultuous sensations which the story of SPOLETO was calculated to inspire in one of his warm temperament, and with feelings, inexperienced before, stirring in the depths of his heart and lending a stern pathos to his tones, he sang:

OUR FLAG.

Must it fall,—our starry flag?
Like a foul dishonored rag,
Shall the daring traitor drag
    It down to rebel dust?
Shall it be a badge of shame,
Or a thing we scorn to name,
Once the emblem of our fame?
    No! Swear we, wave it must!

It has braved the battle-breeze,
It has waved o'er wreck-strewn seas,
While beneath sank conquered knees,
    While flushed the victor's brow;
And o'er ramparts crimson-dyed
With its champions' life-blood tide,
It has flaunted in its pride:
    And must it falter now?

No! Throughout our spreading land,
There is drawing many a brand,
There is pledging heart and hand,
   To guard the ensign well;
And from Maine's snow-crested verge,
To Pacific's billowy surge,
Sternly rings the felon's dirge,—
   Loud tolls the rebel's knell.

By our country's patriot sires,
Whose memory still inspires;
By their cheerless camping fires;
   By the steps they tracked in blood;
By the long years of their strife,
With the deadly bullet rife,
Putting many a busy life
   To rest beneath the sod;

ARLINGTON HEIGHTS.

By the heroes and the sages,
Whose names in coming ages
Shall be traced in history's pages,
    And thrill in hearts unborn;
That flag must never waver—
Nor traitor live to brave her;
We swear to die!—or save her
   From the miscreant's hate and scorn.

Of all the jewels bright
That gleam in clustered light,
Like twinkling orbs at night,
    In COLUMBIA's diadem,
If a single star be lost,
Our blood we would exhaust,
Nor count or pains or cost
    To ransom back the gem.

Though the rushing battle-sleet
Fall like hail about our feet,
Yet who would not leap to greet
    That banner proud unrolled?
And bear it o'er the field,
Till each haughty foe should yield,
And rebellion's fate were sealed,
    Or,—be shrouded in its fold?

As the Lieutenant proceeded, not only his own immediate companions, but group after group, scattered over the heights, caught up the strain, till a thousand sturdy voices,

"Like to the billows' many cadenced sweep,"

rang out the thrilling anthem, waking the night echoes of the woods and startling the distant outposts of the enemy.

The tattoo rang out its warning voice,—again!—and yet again!—and in a short time the Heights were deserted to the challenge of the guardsman, and the wakeful tread of the sentinel.

Softly spread the midnight mists over the noble river: placidly fell the moon's mellowed radiance, like a soft halo, over the now hazy outline of stream and shore: and proudly, proudly as if in conscious power, floated above the scene our country's starry banner

NOTES.

NOTES.

1.—In the morning, the Irish at dawn went to Mass, and, I believe every one of them approached Holy Communion—*Correspondence of the Dublin Post.*

2.—We do not know whether *piety* was not a characteristic of the hero of Clontarf, as well as of GODFREY; or whether RICHARD was not *patriotic* as well as *valiant:* but we have given, as appears to us, the *distinguishing* traits of the three heroes.

3.—Before the battle, Major O'REILLY sent a messenger to the Minister of War, asking assistance for his small force against the overwhelming numbers of the enemy.

4.—"Everywhere has the Society been plundered of its movable property, and real estates. Its members, to the number of about fifteen hundred, have been driven from their establishments, and expelled from the towns in which they lived: they have been escorted by armed bands, like miscreants, from place to place, thrown into public prisons, maltreated, and outrageously insulted. This system of persecutions has gone so far as to prevent them accepting an asylum that the piety of individual families might offer. In many localities no regard whatever has been shown to old age, ill health or infirmity."—*Extract from the Protest of Father Beck, Superior-General of the Jesuits.*

5.—The number of the combatants in the battle of SPOLETO, is variously estimated. The *greatest* given number of the Irish in any of the reports I have seen,—and I have seen many,—is three hundred; the *smallest* given number of tho Piedmontese is eight thousand: even a *greater* disparity than that indicated in the text.

6.—"They, (the Piedmontese,) opened fire from their heavy artillery planted on the small hills around, at a distance at which the old metal in the town was unable to reply."—*London Tablet.*

7.—"At SPOLETO, from early dawn, two gallant brothers, named FLEMING, were on the most exposed part of the wall. About twelve o'clock a bullet killed one, who fell dead on the banquette beside his brother. The survivor, undismayed by his fate, knelt on the dead body of his brother, which enabled him better to reach over the parapet, and continued firing until night."—*Extract from Major O'Reilly's speech at a banquet in Wexford.*

8.—"Two and two make four," or "a quantity added to itself is doubled," is a simple truth. Take it away, and at one stroke you destroy mathematics and all the natural sciences, nearly all the inventions and improvements that are the boast of our age and all the appliances that are the means of preserving human life. If such are the consequences of the suppression of a single *scientific* truth, what will result from suppressing a truth in the *moral* order? Take away the idea that obedience is due to lawfully-constituted and lawfully-administered governments, and you reduce the world to original chaos.

9.—The reader need not be here reminded of the Order for the redemption of captives.

10.—"Return, and tell your commander that we are Irishmen, and that we hold this citadel for God and the Pope. The Irish who serve the Pope are ready to die but not to surrender " *O'Reilly's answer to the flag of truce, verbatim.*

11.—" In poured the besiegers into the outer yard. A bloody reception met them there. The Irish had two guns loaded with grape planted inside in a position commanding the entrance, and no sooner was the Piedmontese column seen through the smoke of the gateway, than a murderous fire was opened, mowing them down literally like corn before the sickle. Again, again, again, the besiegers dashed through the gate ; again, again, and again, a perfect shower of grapeshot met them from the Irish inside."—*Correspondent of the Morning News.*

"Of those who manned the guns, not one escaped. They asked no quarter and they received none : they fought across the carriages of their pieces: they were bayonetted at their posts."—*Ibid.*

12.—"At this juncture, the Papal delegate, with authority that left O'REILLY no resource but obedience, ordered him imperatively to capitulate."—*Dublin Morning News.*

"Monsignor MERODE seeing that the garrison could not hold out for a long time, sent the most positive orders to Major O'REILLY to evacuate."—*Private Letter from Rome.*

www.ingramcontent.com/pod-product-compliance
Lightning Source LLC
Chambersburg PA
CBHW032240080426
42735CB00008B/941